A Gift For:

From:

Published in 2018 by Hallmark Gift Books,
a division of Hallmark Cards, Inc.,
Kansas City, MO 64141
Visit us on the Web at Hallmark.com.

Editorial Director: Delia Berrigan
Art Director: Chris Opheim
Designer: Mark Voss
Production Designer: Dan Horton

ISBN: 978-1-63059-765-8
BOK1091

Made in China
0118

SoulSpa

60 DEVOTIONS FOR REFLECTION, RELAXATION, AND RENEWAL

BY SUSAN DUKE

Introduction

If given the opportunity to visit a spa for a day or for a weeklong stay, we'll soon realize just how much our physical body has needed the attention, tender care, and stress relief. It's easy to get caught up in the daily routines and responsibilities of life and neglect the importance of self-care. Certainly, we can feel the pangs of built-up stress and can easily set an appointment for a therapeutic massage, a facial and mani-pedis, and treat ourselves to a time-out and physical refreshment.

But what about the care our souls need? How often do we ignore the voice of our own soul crying out for relief and nourishment? Our physical bodies know when we are tired, hungry, and thirsty, but how does our soul tell us when it's burned out, thirsty, and starving? I'm reminded of the suggestion that we must put on our own oxygen mask first before we can help someone else. To live our lives fully, we can't ignore the most important and eternal part of us—our soul. If we stop long enough and listen, we'll hear the longing within and hear what our soul is speaking and what it's craving.

The One who created and loves our beautiful and mysterious soul also desires to fill us to overflowing with love and the spiritual nourishment we crave. We just have to be available, spend time with Him, listen for His voice, and soak in the refreshing springs of His care. We can begin by believing and receiving the promise: "He satisfies the thirsty and fills the hungry with good things." Psalm 107:8-10

We all need some soul time, soul space, and soul nourishment of rest and renewal to live our lives fully awake. Inviting awareness and tending our soul will not only revive us and deepen and strengthen us, but also transform us.

If your spirit is weary—and if it's parched and hungry for the things that will quench, nourish, and satisfy it—I invite you to grab a cup of tea, open the next few pages, rest for a while, and find some refreshment for your beautiful soul.

He refreshes my soul.

PSALM 23:3

Something to Celebrate

**We have different gifts, according to
the grace given to each of us.**

ROMANS 12:6

What do bubble baths, bouquets of flowers, seaweed wraps, and hot stone massages have in common? The many kinds of women who love them.

Not only do we express our differences in a myriad of ways, but we stake a claim on our own womanhood and wear our invisible banners of acceptance proudly. It's more than OK to celebrate the uniqueness of who we were created to be. While we all share the reality of being little girls who grew up into women, we see that there is no one kind of woman. Whether she's the type of woman who loves to take off her shoes and walk barefoot in the grass or turns shopping into a party with invited friends or never tires of caring, nurturing, and sharing great stories over afternoon tea—we all can embrace the strengths and abilities that are uniquely our own.

God designed us differently for a divine purpose. While we are entrusted with planting hopes and harvesting dreams, we are also entrusted with embracing the generous joys of being a woman. Perhaps God smiles when we freely celebrate our differences and savor the moments that set us apart. Today and every day, take some time to nurture your beautiful soul and celebrate being you!

Dear God,

Help me remember
that Your plan and purpose
for my life is made complete
by celebrating and being who
You created me to be.

Amen

Beautiful Significance

I praise you because I am fearfully and wonderfully made;
your works are wonderful, I know that full well.

PSALM 139:14

The next time you are in a grocery store checkout line, take a close look at the magazine display rack. Articles about self-improvement, weight loss, beauty, and health advice fill the pages of countless periodicals. Motivational and self-help books rank number one in most bookstores. The target market for this massive onslaught of self-improvement materials is women like you and me who want to look, feel, and be our best.

Making the most of what God has given us is certainly commendable as long as we are careful about not buying into well-meaning but often mixed messages about real confidence. Their primary themes suggest that if we lose enough weight, wear the latest hairstyle, and maybe even have a little plastic surgery, we will exude an acceptable image in society and gain more confidence.

While it's a worthy endeavor to maintain a good physical image, our truest confidence and self-worth will never be found in the mirror or in the eyes of marketing media, regardless of what lengths we are willing to go to on our self-improvement journey.

We were born in search of significance. God has gone to great lengths to assure us of our worth. We are fearfully and wonderfully made. Certainly, He wants us to challenge ourselves physically, mentally, and spiritually. But knowing we are beautifully created turns our focus to the real significance that rests in the center of our soul. Your life and my life matter. We are made in God's image, deeply loved and accepted by the One who affirms we are His chosen and His best.

Dear Lord,

**Thank You for teaching me that true significance
is found in You and for giving me the peace and assurance
that I am valuable and precious to You.**

Amen

Love That Shines

The greatest of these is love.

1 CORINTHIANS 13:13

It's been observed both physically and scientifically that when our hearts and lives are filled with love, there's a certain glow that visibly shines from our eyes and even on our faces. Love is as invisible as the air we breathe, and equally essential. The Bible affirms that it's even greater than hope or faith. Love has inspired poets, songwriters, and philosophers for decades. The miracle and mystery of love remain indescribable, but love is the most fulfilling and complete gift God has ever given us.

Because of the romantic symbols we use to celebrate Valentine's Day, we often forget that St. Valentine actually lost his life because of his love for God. Long before St. Valentine was adopted as the patron saint of lovers, he clearly knew that God's love was the foundation of true love. The soul-deep and abiding love that fills our hearts has the power to overflow and channel into every aspect of our lives. The kind of love Christ has sacrificed for you and me came in human form to demonstrate and unite our hearts to God's.

We have the sacred bliss and gift of love to celebrate every single day. Certainly, we can physically create an outward glow with the right herbal facial mask or professional facial treatment, but nothing compares to the radiance and glow that shines outwardly from the love within our soul.

Dear God,

Thank You for wrapping me in Your love
and for perfecting it in me and through me.
Help me remember that love is what fills and shines
from the deepest part of my soul.

Amen

Soul Vision

**For the revelation awaits an appointed time;
it speaks of the end and will not prove false.
Though it linger, wait for it; it will certainly come.**

HABAKKUK 2:3

It's easy to become disheartened when life simply doesn't line up with our dreams or expectations. Our dreams and our vision can easily get lost beneath the daily complexities of life. We may even tell ourselves we are foolish to believe in something greater than our current situations.

Do you have a vision for what you desire your life to look like? God also has a vision for our lives. Much like the process of a wonderful pedicure, we anticipate and envision the finished result—after the soaking, trimming, filing, and buffing our beautiful feet had to go through first.

Our own visions are tested in our hearts, held up to the light of God's will, and then filtered to fit His plan for our lives. God encourages us to hold on to our vision and write it down. Keeping it before us reminds us that we shouldn't become discouraged while the process of our dream or vision is taking place.

From Genesis to Revelation, we find many who questioned God's plan and their own vision during times of waiting. God always brought forth the promise and vision that originated from Him. Psalm 16:3 (AMPC) reminds us: "Roll your works upon the Lord [commit and trust them wholly to Him; He will cause your thoughts to become agreeable to His will, and] so shall your plans be established and succeed."

When a dream or vision seed is planted deeply within our soul, we can trust that God's timing will unfold and our vision will be fulfilled.

Dear God,

I will hold fast to my vision and dreams,
even when it looks like they won't come to pass.
Help me trust that Your vision for my life is far greater
than any I can dream or imagine.

Amen

Using Our Eyes, Hands, Feet, and Hearts

Be kind and compassionate to one another.

EPHESIANS 4:32

Sometimes, a single word will seem irrelevant to our active, personal needs. And yet, words like "compassion" mean so much when we're the ones in need. Compassion is stronger and deeper than caring. It's more than observation. Compassion is never a random act of charity or kind gesture of obligation. Compassion was and is the very heart of God. Our eyes, our hands, our feet, and our hearts are the conduits of both receiving and giving compassion. Jesus's heart was moved with compassion whenever He encountered someone in physical or emotional pain. He didn't offer superficial answers or solutions; but He met people in the depths of their suffering. He fed them, ate with them, listened to the cries of their hearts, and most importantly, He wept with them.

Perhaps, we understand the importance of this deeper caring after we've been the one whose soul was in desperate need of a listening ear, a hand of practical help, or an understanding offer of grace. One of our soul's greatest missions is to be a vessel God trusts to pour out His compassion. We pay forward what we've been given when we are willing to be His hands, His feet, His eyes, and His heart. When one word, such as compassion, becomes active, it becomes a miracle that changes lives and brings healing to those broken places we all experience in this life.

Heavenly Father,

As Your compassion fills me
and brings healing to my soul,
move me with the same kind of compassion
that moved You to help others.

Amen

The Real Me

**Before I formed you in the womb I knew you,
before you were born I set you apart.**

JEREMIAH 1:5

Authenticity is probably one of the healthiest attributes anyone can have. And yet, as women, we often fall into the trap of seeking out role models we can't possibly pattern ourselves after. We strive for physical self-improvements with time at the gym or trying out the latest health spa therapies, like a hot stone massage or herbal body wrap, hoping to boost our self-confidence. But what matters most is exploring and becoming consistently real. We set ourselves up for stress if we are one way in public and completely different with close friends or family.

Perhaps there's someone who genuinely exemplifies our idea of a well-balanced or Godly woman. Maybe she's more organized, dresses like a fashion model, or has the best exercise and diet disciplines. Following a great example is certainly a good thing. But trying to copy someone else to the degree that we lose our sense of authenticity is unhealthy.

God designed each of us to be unique—and for a purpose. The part of us that tends to be a little more spontaneous (making it hard to have it all together all the time) and our funny little quirks set us apart, define us, and give us our distinct personalities.

Healthy soul-searching takes time to ask ourselves a few questions about our truest selves. Who is the real me—after the hot stone massage, beneath the body wrap, without makeup, after I kick off my high heels, or change into my pajamas? What moves my soul? What is my heart's desire, my deepest passion, my greatest need? What dreams do I dare dream when no one is looking? Who am I in the middle of change and challenges?

There is true freedom in being real! Celebrating the uniqueness of our authenticity allows us to be and do and fulfill our very own created purpose as God's masterpiece.

Dear Lord,

Give me the courage to be real and to embrace exactly who You created me to be.

Amen

Prayerful Promise

Christ Jesus . . . is at the right hand of God and is also interceding for us.

ROMANS 8:34

There will always be times when we feel like our prayers barely reach the ceiling, much less reach God. It's easy to feel defeated or weak and powerless when we can't muster the words we need to speak and believe. That's when words from a friend who says "I'll be praying for you" mean the most. It's OK to admit we aren't strong when we're fighting our way out of a hurtful situation or life-altering event. Grieving over a lost loved one or a marriage that has ended in divorce, or the concern for a wayward child challenges our greatest prayerful attempts.

I heard a very short example a few years ago that changed my way of thinking about the times when I can't find the words or the power behind my prayers. An old woman who was known as an intercessor told a younger woman who was crying because she was hurting too deeply to pray: "Honey, it's OK. Just let Jesus pray."

Isn't it nice to know that when we physically need some spa time to let the professionals work their magic, all we have to do is simply be there and relax? What a beautiful respite for our soul when we realize we can relax and simply turn everything over to Jesus and know that He is praying and working out everything on our behalf.

Dear Lord,

Knowing I'm never far from Your thoughts
brings rest and comfort to my soul.
Thank You for personally loving me enough
to pray when I can't find the words.

Amen

Brave Heart

Be strong and take heart and wait for the Lord.

PSALM 27:14

There's a defining difference between being a strong woman and being a woman of strength. A strong woman is dependent on outward resources and abilities. We can stretch and tone our muscles through exercise and massage sessions to become a stronger woman. But a woman of strength relies on an inner strength that is always accessible. It's been said that we are truly spiritual beings who experience things humanly, and those human battles we face are best fought from our spiritual selves.

We don't have to be Wonder Woman or a superhero to fight on the front lines of life's battlefields. In the biblical story, the great giant, Goliath, must have laughed when he saw the young lad, David, who had come to take him down. Although he towered above little David, he was no match for the relentless strength of a believing soul. He underestimated David's heart of bravery and forgot to factor in David's inner strength—his faith in God.

Courage and bravery prevail when our cause is greater than our fear! The more we stretch our faith, the stronger spiritually we become. We can face the giants in our lives with a brave heart, confident that Jesus, the real hero of every battle, is walking beside us helping us be victorious. Strong souls are courageous souls that partner with a brave heart and step fearlessly beyond the obstacles of life.

Dear God,

Thank You for making my soul strong and my heart brave. When the giants of life appear, give me faith to face them without fear.

Amen

9

Progressive Patience

**Let perseverance finish its work
so that you may be mature and complete,
not lacking anything.**

JAMES 1:4

I remember my mother telling me (more than a few times) that all worthwhile things in life take time. But, we live in a society of demanding and expecting what we want immediately. We thrive on convenience. Fast food, fast internet, and bite-sized messages and abbreviations for words are the ways of texts and social media. Incidents of road rage triple every year. People aren't patient enough to exercise common driving courtesies.

Certain things in life and in our walk with God simply can't be rushed. A paraphrased quote I spied on a gymnasium wall read, "We should never sacrifice the quality of what's permanent on the altar of the immediate." In rushing ahead of God's timing, we settle for a fast food meal of satisfaction rather than the nutritious, slow-cooked food for our soul He'd like to serve us. Spiritual malnutrition is an unsavory and costly price to pay for convenience.

In a self-serving world, a refresher course in the art of patience and long-suffering might be a good way to revisit the fruits of the spirit. Anyone who serves God has always gone through a process of testing and timing. Joseph endured rejection from his own family and was left for dead. There were no instant answers for Joseph. In time, God raised him up, honored him, and even gave him the compassion to help the very family who had betrayed him.

God will go to great lengths to make sure we don't sacrifice His plan for immediate answers. Trusting His timing establishes patience and lasting peace for our soul.

Dear God,

As You unfold the details of Your plan for my life,
let my soul find peace through learning to trust Your timing.

Amen

Clear Direction

**Whether you turn to the right or to the left,
your ears will hear a voice behind you, saying,
"This is the way; walk in it."**

ISAIAH 30:21

Anytime we venture down the highway into unknown territory, we need to study and highlight our driving path. Traveling on vacation by car requires a good map. But even great planning for our destination doesn't always prepare us for what's not on the map, like unforeseen detours and unfamiliar roads. Our sense of direction can be greatly altered by anything that is not clearly marked on the map.

When we make new plans to take better care of ourselves, we seek out a health guide; we make commitments and appointments, and follow directions. When Moses led the children of Israel through the wilderness, he didn't have a paper map to rely on. Can you imagine leading thousands of people into unknown territory without knowing the terrain? It was certainly no vacation having to rely on heavenly food to feed the masses of people or on the cloud by day that kept them from scorching in the sun or on the fire by night to keep them warm. God provided everything that was needed for the journey through the wilderness; and yet, some still doubted God's power and strength when they heard giants were waiting in the Promised Land. Moses trusted God's direction, and regardless of what happened along the way, He remained on God's path.

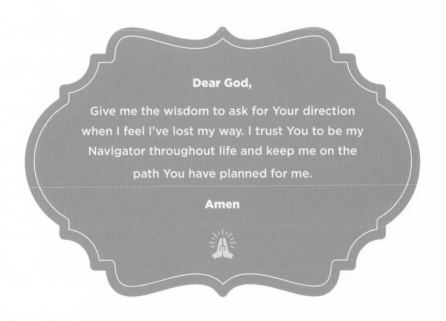

Dear God,

Give me the wisdom to ask for Your direction when I feel I've lost my way. I trust You to be my Navigator throughout life and keep me on the path You have planned for me.

Amen

11

Taking Time to Love Yourself

"Teacher, which is the greatest commandment in the Law?"
Jesus replied: "'Love the Lord your God with all your heart
and with all your soul and with all your mind.' This is the first
and greatest commandment. And the second is like it:
'Love your neighbor as yourself.'"

MATTHEW 22:36-39

It's easy for any of us get so caught up in life's daily urgencies that we ignore the voice of our own souls crying out for rest and relief. While we gladly fulfill our duties and responsibilities that need tending, too many hours and days without a break can leave us feeling weary, frazzled, and overwhelmed. We nonchalantly chalk up our agendas to a normal way of living, right? After all, it's who we are and what we do. And we're thankful for a full life. But if we're honest with ourselves, we will likely recognize a very real inward struggle between balancing life's daily cares and caring for ourselves.

If we continually ignore our internal need for breathing space, refreshment, and physical, mental, and spiritual renewal, we'll eventually burn out. Balance and self-renewal require diligently paying attention to our own personal spiritual, physical, and mental needs. Learning to love ourselves is not always a priority, but perhaps, God's most beautiful secret of living our lives to the fullest is found in Jesus's second greatest instruction of loving others as *we love ourselves.*

Dear God,

Humbly remind me and teach me that loving others

is best achieved by also loving myself.

Amen

Who Am I?

I am my beloved's and my beloved is mine.

SONG OF SONGS 6:3

Sometimes, because of comparisons, or because we tend to label ourselves by what we do, our perspective of who we are becomes dimmed or diminished. That's when we need to check in with our heart and remind ourselves that we are more than our past, our circumstances, or how we feel emotionally. We are not defined by our age or a number on the scale. If we want to encourage a friend, we speak such affirming words as: You are brave, you are beautiful, and you are strong. These are the very words we need to also believe and speak to ourselves.

When we add our own name to our to-do lists, we remind ourselves that we are valuable enough to care for ourselves. Taking time-outs and mini-breaks (or really big ones) keeps us rejuvenated and balanced in our everyday living. We can't do everything or be all things for everyone all the time. When what we do flows from who we are, we tap into the empowerment needed to accomplish and do the things that truly matter.

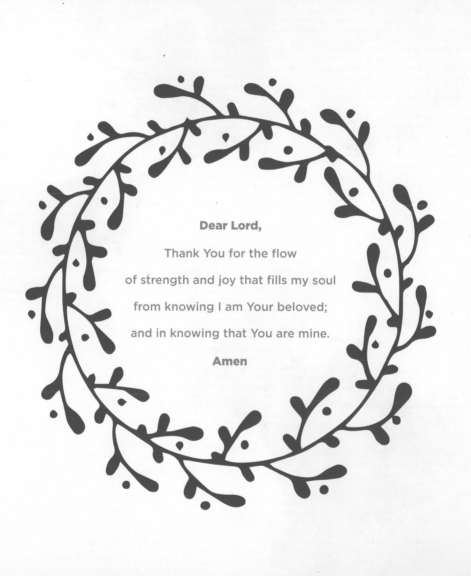

Dear Lord,

Thank You for the flow

of strength and joy that fills my soul

from knowing I am Your beloved;

and in knowing that You are mine.

Amen

13

Empowered Excellence

We have this treasure in jars of clay to show that this all-surpassing power is from God and not from us.

2 CORINTHIANS 4:7

Spending time at a beauty salon, getting our nails manicured, making strategic plans for eating right, and searching for the latest beauty tips are all commendable goals for achieving and portraying self-confidence.

Adopting new routines, joining a gym, making healthy diet choices, and scheduling a massage are lifestyle habits and changes that take willpower, structure, and consistency. Each or all of these will improve our well-being, and we will see the visible results of our aspirations; but beneath the temporary fixes of outward appearances is the real goal of feeling our best from within. True and steady confidence comes from a deeper awareness and soul-assurance that our very human and physical bodies house something magnificent!

In our desire for excellence, there is one beautiful truth that outshines our physical needs. Within each of us resides *His* "personal best"—the excellency of power—*God Himself.* The greatest confidence we'll ever need.

Heavenly Father,

Give me more awareness of who You are inside of me;
and let Your excellence empower and flow through me.

Amen

An Ever-Present Hope

Whatever is true, whatever is noble, whatever is right, whatever is pure, whatever is lovely, whatever is admirable—if anything is excellent or praiseworthy—think about such things.

PHILIPPIANS 4:8

Have you ever had a series of days, months, or years that became an entire season of sorrow or discontent because of challenging situations? These are the times when we wonder if we'll make it through a financial struggle, a critical illness, a soul-crushing disappointment or betrayal, the death of a loved one, or a broken relationship. Some hurts are so deep, the process so great, we question everything we've ever believed or trusted. Our thoughts and emotions shift. We view life from a new perspective. Why? Because we've never been here before. We've never walked this path or been prepared to deal with the unknowns of life. When we land here, we make choices about our responses to a new kind of normal.

A dear friend who'd undergone months of chemotherapy made sure afterwards to continue her health routine by focusing on self-care with regular visits to a spa for soothing essential oil massages and time to relax in an atmosphere of soft music. It combined her physical needs with a quiet time to pray, meditate, and renew her hope.

One thing is certain: In the shifting shadows of life, we can choose to focus on the darkness or to look for the light. It's a work of our heart and soul to deliberately search out the good in every single day. Brokenness will either entrap us or free us to find our soul's deepest truth and beauty. When we look for glimpses of hope and God's grace, we may find it takes us closer and deeper than we've ever been to His heart. Jesus, through His message of life and love, challenged us to look at simple blessings and learn from them. If we listen, we'll hear the voice that rises and speaks through the ashes of shattered dreams, calling us to embrace and think about the gift each day brings.

Dear Lord,

Despite how my life looks and feels right now, I choose to think good thoughts about the blessings, promises, and hope waiting in each new sunrise.

Amen

15

A Basin and a Towel

**Let a little water be brought,
and then you may all wash your feet.**

GENESIS 18:4

Do you remember those first days of summer as a child when you finally had permission to go barefoot and feel the lush, green grass beneath your little feet? Perhaps you even painted your toenails a bold color to celebrate the summer season.

We never outgrow the need to feel that freedom of bare feet, perhaps after a long day at work or when we get home from grocery shopping. Maybe we long to put our tired and aching feet in some cool water or soak them in a foot basin filled with fragrant and soothing bath salts.

In biblical days, because nearly everyone walked to their destinations (most likely in open sandals), people's feet naturally got dusty and dirty. As an act of hospitality, respect, and care, it was a common practice in homes to keep a basin and towel ready to wash a weary traveler's feet when they arrived.

Today, our feet are shielded from the elements of dusty roads. But a simple indulgence of refreshing our tired, bare feet is still a beautiful thing we can do for ourselves, whether that be through a long soak or a full pedicure. It can also serve as a reminder that we are always free to come barefoot before God, just as we are, in need of refreshing for our dusty soul, and know He is waiting with His basin and towel of grace to wash away our weariness.

Dear Lord,

Thank You for all the ways
you show me You care and for reminding me
that Your love washes away the dust
and the weariness from my soul.

Amen

16

What the Soul Craves

"The Lord made the heavens. Splendor and majesty are before him; strength and glory are in his sanctuary."

PSALM 96:5-6

Wonder. We were born with it. And it served us well in childhood, evidenced by the awe of stargazing or catching magical fireflies in a mason jar. As teenagers, and still in young adulthood, it motivated our sense of adventure about life and living. And then, with all of its grown-up challenges, real life happened, and we lost it—or, at the very least, misplaced it. Our God-given sense of wonder diminished in the pressing realities that allowed little time for such things as pondering or engaging in nature or creation. Wonder is something our soul naturally craves. It's that part of our soul that wants to come out and play and bask in the amazement of nature and beauty.

Sometimes, we have to set our own soul free again. Perhaps we don't realize what we've been missing until we find it once more. But when we do, it's like finding lost treasure. If we will sit and watch a sunset for a few nights, we'll accept the front row seat provided just for us by God, the Master Artist. We'll not only witness an amazing display of colorful brilliance and beauty, we'll experience the miracle and the majesty of oneness with God . . . and all of creation. We can't allow the sacredness of wonder to disappear. It's part of us, and it's a gift from our Creator. Wonder is alive and well inside of us. We just have to invite it forth from the depths of our soul and savor the priceless richness it brings to our life.

Dear God,

Help me remember that wonder is sacred and ageless.

Keep me listening for the whisper in my soul of Holy praise and celebration

for the miracles of Your glorious creation.

Amen

One Thing

Martha was distracted by all the preparations that had to be made.
She came to him and asked, "Lord, don't you care that my sister has left me to
do the work by myself? Tell her to help me!"
"Martha, Martha," the Lord answered, "you are worried and upset about
many things, but few things are needed—or indeed only one.
Mary has chosen what is better, and it will not be taken away from her."

LUKE 10:40-42

I don't know about you, but so often, I find myself answering someone who asks how I'm doing with one word: busy. Truthfully, we all tend to interpret busy lives as full lives. The Chinese word for "busyness" combines two symbols made of these two words: heart killer. Someone once said that we are not called to a busyness that drains us but to an abundance that trains us. Now, there's a soul-searching thought to ponder! Taking time to evaluate what is power driven, stress driven, or what is truly heart-and-soul driven inside of ourselves is a game changer. One of the best things we can do for our own well-being is to take inventory of what truly fills us up. When we declutter our closets, we find that less actually is more, that simplicity is freeing. When we declutter our souls and untangle our hearts, we discover the powerful peacekeeping secret that keeps us centered, balanced, and free from the trappings of busy-driven lives.

There is "one thing" that is genuinely powerful and that trumps any kind of earthly power we think we need for our daily existence. In scripture, the story of Martha's busyness being compared to Mary's lingering at the feet of Jesus clearly reminds us of "the one thing" that will truly satisfy our soul and help us live fulfilled lives: taking time with God.

Dear Lord,

I so desire to end the cycle of busyness in my life that takes time away from experiencing Your presence. Help me learn the art of being versus always doing.

Amen

18

Taking Time to Refuel

He said to them, "Come with me by yourselves
to a quiet place and get some rest."

MARK 6:31

There's nothing quite like a personal adventure to change up our daily routine. It may include a day trip down the back roads or visiting a shop or restaurant where we've never been. Sometimes, we need new views and scenery to motivate our creativity and invite new discoveries, perceptions, and perspectives. These are the deliberately planned and set-apart moments that can nurture and refresh our soul. Driving time can become a much needed prayer time without distractions. Giving ourselves time and permission to get off the beaten path rests us spiritually, emotionally, mentally, and physically. A little retail therapy might not hurt either! Stopping to not only smell the wayside flowers, but also to pick a few to take home and place on our kitchen table are the little, often-ignored blessings available to us every day.

A full calendar may be exciting, but too many days without a break to regroup and recharge will land us in burnout mode. Jesus was a people person and surrounded by many who needed His teaching and care; but the human part of Him needed and allowed himself times of solitude to break away and be refueled and refilled. In our quest for living an abundant life, we need to remember that our soul needs balance, wisdom, inspiration, and protection for staying centered. That includes the real stuff of life that is vital to our well-being. God has a bounty of daily blessings and gifts that He longs to deliver to us at the doorsteps of our hearts. We simply need to take time to open the door and unwrap the gift.

Heavenly Father,

As I live my daily life, keep me aware of my need for solitude
and changing up my routine. Help me to step out of my comfort zone
so I might discover the hidden blessings of wayside moments.

Amen

19

Holy Wrappings

Therefore, the promise comes by faith, so that it may be by grace
and may be guaranteed to all Abraham's offspring—
not only to those who are of the law but also to those who have
the faith of Abraham. He is the father of us all.

ROMANS 4:16

I had no idea the many benefits of a seaweed wrap until I experienced one for myself. If our skin could speak, it would surely speak gratitude for this nourishing gift of sea salts, seaweed, amino acids, vitamins, and gentle caring. Do you know that despite what things look or feel like, God has a gift for you? It may not seem true, but there is redemption on the tough days of living and in the shadows of bittersweet celebrations. Jesus assures us that what we unwrap and find beneath the confetti of what should be is the gift of what will always be.

Sometimes, life's offerings may not look like good or tangible gifts; but they are gifts that land in the gift box of our hearts. When opened, there is love. And love always comes packaged in the holy wrappings of promise. The promise that one day things will be set right again, that the dark stain of disappointment won't always color our days, that this time of questioning will be as an instant. A blink when our mourning is turned to dancing. When answers won't be so important anymore. When our tears will be wiped away. When joy finally arrives in the morning, our hearts will reveal in shining splendor what has been there all along.

Love that never dies.
Miraculous hope attained.
Glorious days.
The gift.
The unwrapped promise.
Heaven's treasure.
Today and always.

Dear Lord,

When I'm too afraid to open my heart, fearing what I'll find,
give me faith to unwrap Your waiting gift of promise.

Amen

Simple Pleasures

For with you is the fountain of life; in your light we see light.

PSALM 36:9

No formulas or therapists can nurture our soul like the gift of simplicity. It cowers from the clutter of agendas, and it sets a table of joy, hope, love, and pleasures, sometimes enjoyed with a friend and sometimes by ourselves. But simplicity isn't something that's dropped into our laps. We have to tune our soul to the voice that calls us back to the basics of all things meaningful.

Listen to the longing. Think about simple things you love to do. Do you love curling up in an old quilt by a crackling fire? When is the last time you stepped outside just to marvel at the beauty of a crimson sunset? How long has it been since you walked barefoot along a warm, sandy beach? Counted stars? Perhaps the smell of a fresh apple pie baking in the oven or the feel of gentle soft snowflakes falling on your face warms your soul. An afternoon of book reading, a long bubble bath soak in the tub, and taking the time to go through old photo albums are just a few things that we rarely give ourselves permission to enjoy. Think about a song you love—and sing it or play it. What memories come through the melody? What's your favorite season, and what are the sweet remembrances spent with friends and loved ones that you cherish?

God wants us to enjoy our life. The pathways that lead to resting places for our soul can only be found in the simple, soul-nourishing graces of endearment. When we trace our steps to the places of light where our soul feels most at home, we'll discover that the little things in life truly are our greatest blessings.

Dear God,

Keep me aware of the beautiful gifts of life's simple pleasures. You are giver of life and what nourishes my soul. Keep me rooted and grounded in You and all that I cherish most.

Amen

The Road Ahead

Open my eyes that I may see wonderful things.

PSALM 119:18

While driving one afternoon to Heaven's Touch Massage, one of my favorite places to visit, clear my mind, and let my friend (and the owner) work her magic on my weary muscles, I passed this road sign: "Rough Road Ahead." My first thought: I've been down plenty of those! I know all about rough roads.

Sure enough, the road I was traveling that day became very rough and bumpy. But it didn't matter because I knew what was waiting at my destination was worth the delay and inconvenience. Not once did I think of turning back or getting off the road I was on to look for an easier route.

After I'd finally arrived and positioned myself on the massage table, I immediately felt a sense of calm. My focus turned to the peaceful lighting, sounds, and setting that helped me shut out all of the reasons that had brought me there:

Too much stress. Too many deadlines. Too many responsibilities and insurmountable challenges. The warm lotion and therapeutic touch upon my back reminded me that the rough road I'd traveled to get there was worth it.

I was also reminded of God's presence—and the warm experience of His grace and comfort whenever I set the time to be with Him. Surely, it doesn't just happen. We prepare and plan and create the setting for a sacred appointment. We may have to travel some rough roads before we finally arrive; but the touches of heaven waiting to soothe and refresh our soul are worth it all.

Dear Lord,

Keep me on the road that leads me to Your presence.
Don't let me be tempted by an easier or smoother path;
but help me focus on the joyous bliss of experiencing
Your comfort and tender grace.

Amen

The Gift of Priority

**Seek first his kingdom and his righteousness,
and all these things will be given to you as well.**

MATTHEW 6:33

Priorities reveal much about our lifestyles, our character, and what is most important to us. "First things first" is a phrase often coined for putting and keeping our daily priorities in order. It's vital that in the midst of looming schedules and critical deadlines, we don't miss the most important priority of all: Keeping God first. Life's second most important priority is our relationships. Remaining flexible in our daily priorities is not a lack of self-discipline. It's having a plan, but giving God and others first precedence in our lives. It's not living on the frays of whims; it's allowing our soul the flexibility of remembering and doing what matters most.

While housework is important, cherished time with our children trumps all. We may become so busy in church duties, callings, or careers that we leave no room for what our soul needs most. It is one thing to fill a pew at church—and quite another to spend intimate time at Jesus's feet, allowing Him to refill our soul. The statistics are staggering concerning ministers who have become estranged from their families because they placed their position in the church above their position as husband or parent. Putting things we do for God first is not the same as putting Him first.

Surrendering our agendas and personally inviting the God who sings and delights over us to be first and walk with us throughout our soul's journey set everything else we need in place. Spending time in His presence is not our gift to Him. It's His gift to us.

Dear Lord,

**Help me remember that putting You first
is not a Sunday choice but a daily choice.
Remind me, when I become too rigid in my
well-constructed plans, to keep You and others first.**

Amen

23

A Life That Matters

I have set you an example that you should do as I have done for you.
Very truly I tell you, no servant is greater than his master.

JOHN 13:15-16

While reading a story recently about a woman who had a near-death experience, the part that moved me the most was about how drastically her attitude toward life had changed. Before her experience, she lived to work. She was successful and had money, a great business reputation, and a family she loved. Tears fell down her cheeks as she admitted there'd always seemed to be something missing. When she realized she was going to live, an awareness of life's meaning became extremely clear. Her passion became serving others less fortunate in life. She started a foundation and ministry to help feed and clothe the homeless. She used her connections to hold charitable fundraising events. Her life's mission is to serve others and change lives. She is now happier than she's ever been.

There are multitudes of ways to physically improve ourselves and our lives, but nothing compares to the deep soul-knowing that *our life matters*.

There is no more beautiful picture of servanthood than when Christ met with his disciples to celebrate the Passover the night before he was betrayed. He knelt as a humble servant before his disciples and washed their feet. Such love and compassion became an example of what it means to live with purpose. Galatians 5:13 affirms that we've been given the *freedom* to serve others. Our soul is never truly filled unless it is also free. Your life matters. And with a heart's desire to serve others, we have the beautiful honor of touching and changing lives . . . and changing our own.

Dear God,

I want my life to matter. Show me where I am needed and make me aware of the lives I have an opportunity to help, change, and heal.

Amen

Attitude Adjustments

Be made new in the attitude of your minds.

EPHESIANS 4:23

A little soaking time in a hot bathtub full of bubbles can be a valuable opportunity to stop and give our thoughts a little soaking time, too. Reflecting on the good things in our life, what we need to change, and how our attitudes affect others is a vital treatment for our soul.

Famous for his motivational speaking and training seminars, Zig Ziglar routinely addressed something called "stinking thinking." He believed our well-being, our successes, our failures, and our relationships are all established by how and what we think.

Our attitudes have the power to change and affect the atmosphere where we are and who we're around. If we demonstrate healthy attitudes and responses to life's challenges to our children, family, and friends, more likely than not, those in our inner circle will reflect at least a portion of those same attitudes.

Do naturally optimistic people ever feel disappointed? Certainly, life is full of disappointments that can cause any of us to become jaded and pessimistic about living, but God gives us the ability to train our thought life and vision for living.

While we may not consider attitude adjustments a beauty treatment, a beautifully tweaked attitude will always outshine our outward appearance and reflect the beauty of our soul.

Dear God,

Change my attitude when it needs to be adjusted. When I'm tempted to be pessimistic, remind me of the good things in my life with an attitude of praise and thankfulness.

Amen

Just Show Up

Not that I have already obtained all this, or have already arrived at my goal,
but I press on to take hold of that for which Christ Jesus took hold of me.

PHILIPPIANS 3:12

There will always be days when we don't feel like crawling out of bed, much less showing up for everything we need to project the appearance of having it all together. Some days . . . we just don't. We feel off kilter emotionally, mentally, and physically. And we have no energy to fake anything else. But here's the good news about all that: God knows the good, the bad, and ugly about us. No need to pretend or try to be something we can't pull off on certain days.

The days when we feel like giving up on ourselves are the kinds of days we need to lean against His strength, lay our head on His shoulder, and hear Him say, "It's OK." Some days, showing up is enough. We need to take ourselves off the hook every now and then, put our hair up in a messy bun, lay in a hammock and listen to music, or go to the gym, a spa, or a park and swing. Sometimes, if we're peopled out, that's exactly what our soul needs.

Ironically, by making one simple decision—to just show up—good and unexpected things we couldn't have planned tend to happen. New ideas are born. We run into someone we know we were meant to meet. When time slows down, we catch up with our own runaway heart. And finally, we find ourselves hearing what God's been longing to whisper to our soul:

Come just as you are.

Anytime you need to come.

There's freedom here.

Just show up.

Dear Lord,

Teach my soul that showing up is sometimes enough because any day with You is never wasted.

Amen

Amazed by Grace

**God is able to bless you abundantly,
so that in all things at all times, having all that you need,
you will abound in every good work.**

2 CORINTHIANS 9:8

Grace moments happen often when we least expect them. When it seems impossible that our broken heart will survive another day or wonder if anyone cares, grace leaves a yellow sunshine gift basket filled with lotions, pedicure treats, and a gift card to a local day spa at your door. The note from an anonymous friend simply says, "A treat for your weary feet, from someone who is walking beside you."

When disappointment closes the book on our dream, grace writes a new beginning across our heart. Grace is love personified—a gift with no strings attached. Grace is a glimpse of God's glory in the midst of life's toughest battles. God's cocoon of grace holds us while waiting to emerge from the darkness of grief.

Grace has many faces. But none is sweeter than the face of a friend who reaches far enough and stays long enough to walk with us through the valley of brokenness. When all hope disappears and we've exhausted our own strength, like an oasis in a desert, grace shows up.

No matter what stains have marked our past, grace finds us and wipes the slate clean. In the realm of God's all-powerful grace, we are restored and saturated in His mercy. His grace resounds with this simple truth: There is nothing we can do to make God love us less, and nothing we do can make Him love us more than He already does right now. That's why grace is so amazing.

Heavenly Father,

Thank You for never giving up on me—even when I do.
Your unconditional love and amazing grace carry me, soothe me,
and bring healing to my soul.

Amen

Priceless Conditions

How precious to me are your thoughts, God!
How vast is the sum of them!

PSALM 139:17

One day while looking for a good used car in the classifieds, I was intrigued and amused at all the descriptions. My first thought was how many of us might describe ourselves in similar fashion: Lots of miles, but still in good shape! Garage kept! In fair condition! Service regularly maintained! Good tires! Rebuilt engine! Great gas mileage! Clean with a few dents! Needs some TLC. Old but dependable.

I couldn't help but think how we could relate to a few of these labels! Our physical and spiritual conditions become part of our identity. And sadly, we often take better care of our cars than we do ourselves. I remember a song from more than a few years back that talked about seeing what condition our condition is in. And perhaps we need to do that very thing!

I wonder what our own classified ad might look like—in need of a deep body and soul massage, a little aromatherapy to wake up the senses, an application of essential oil to soften the body, and the oil of the Holy Spirit to soften the soul.

God gives us all we need to keep our soul in good condition. He maintains us with His atoning love—and He will never give us up. If we asked Him to place a description of us in the classifieds, it might read something like this: Treasured, highly favored, blessed, adored, beautiful, beloved, and priceless. Not for sale. Ever.

Precious Lord,

Thank You,
for caring for all of me,
and for maintaining
and sustaining my soul
with Your love and grace.

Amen

Watchful Soul

**Come and see what God has done,
his awesome deeds for mankind!**

PSALM 66:5

God, the Master Artist, gave us nature to enjoy and savor. Just as we look for the meaning in the artwork of the old art masters, our Master Artist wants us to step into the painting He has created for our pleasure. Look and see. Observe. Think. Delight in the little things that often go unnoticed in our everyday living.

When was the last time you took some time to bask in God's wondrous bounty and truly allowed yourself to be caught up in the wonder of God's magnificent handiwork? Have you gazed lately at God's suspended curtain of dancing stars displayed against a midnight sky?

Did you know your soul can harmonize with the song of a rippling brook?

Insight unearths the treasure of bliss we knew as a child when our eyes were keen with expectation. It connects us to the splendor of our Creator. It takes us to a place of reflection, awe, and reverence for God's majesty in our lives.

God has given us beautiful gifts to refresh our heart and open our eyes to the everyday miracles He will paint across the canvas of our soul.

Dear God,

I want to live my life inspired by the bountiful beauty
You've created for my enjoyment and refreshment.
As the Master Artist of my soul, paint my life
with the colors of Your love.

Amen

Trusting God's Will

"For I know the plans I have for you," declares the Lord,
"plans to prosper you and not to harm you,
plans to give you hope and a future."

JEREMIAH 29:11

Learning to trust God's will for our life is a little like finding a plain brown box filled with pieces of a jigsaw puzzle. We sometimes wonder where all the pieces of our life fit together in God's plan, and we may get anxious or impatient when trying to see the complete picture. There are fragments of life that just don't seem to fit what we've hoped it would be.

Sorting through countless pieces, we often ask God what His will is for us. The answer doesn't always come immediately. It's only when we pick up each piece, hold it up to God, and ask Him to show us how the pieces fit that we catch a partial glimpse of His plan and will.

We often know something is physically wrong, but we need medical or professional help to see the whole picture. A chiropractor or a masseuse can feel what needs to be properly lined up or put back into place. God is always working and transforming our will to His, reworking and placing each piece of our life's puzzle into place. Our job is to simply trust that He knows exactly where every piece of the puzzle fits.

Dear God,

I choose to trust the mountainous view
of Your perspective for my life. I give You the
pieces of my heart and soul that feel fragmented
and ask You to place them in the picture
of Your plan for me.

Amen

Simply Well With My Soul

I urge . . . that prayers . . . be made for all people, that we may live peaceful and quiet lives in all godliness and holiness.

1 TIMOTHY 2:1-2

Do you find yourself longing for a less complicated, less frantic way of living? Yearning for simpler living as in days gone by?

If you ever wonder if simplicity has become a lost art, you're not alone. For the past few years, there's been a sort of simplicity renaissance. Bookstore shelves are filled with books and magazines about simplifying and downsizing our lives.

Jesus warned His followers and warns us about the trappings of this world. He came with a simple message: life. He had one single motive: love. The Pharisees didn't understand His simplicity or His disregard for what they deemed religious. They contrived, manipulated, and complicated every simple parable He spoke. They declared their rules, their buildings, and their rituals as true religion.

If we are not focused on simplicity, we miss what really counts—Christ's personal, heart-to-heart relationship with us. Simplicity implores us to be more about "being" than "doing." He calls us the living stones—His dwelling place.

There's a higher ground of rest for our souls where we can take refuge from the clutter and noise of this world. It's a place where the gentle voice of simplicity calls us to do a little porch sitting, share a story and some laughter, and enjoy some friendship moments over iced tea . . . or maybe even share a few tears. The stuff life is made of. Simply well with my soul.

Heavenly Father,

Unclutter my soul so it will hear and follow the voice of simplicity.

Forgive me for the things and ways of thinking I've allowed

to complicate my life and my walk with You.

Amen

Pushing Through, Pressing On

Not only so, but we also glory in our sufferings,
because we know that suffering produces perseverance;
perseverance, character; and character, hope.

ROMANS 5:3-4

The first time I walked out of a day spa I remember thinking that I just needed to go home and go to bed! I wasn't at all sure the discomfort of such intense muscle stimulation was worth it. My muscles ached and felt stretched beyond what I'd thought would be a comforting experience. The following day found me feeling surprisingly flexible and rejuvenated!

When our faith muscles are stretched beyond our own understanding and limitations, our faith is made stronger to persevere through the next challenges ahead.

It was perseverance that motivated the woman in the Bible who suffered from bleeding to press in and touch the hem of Jesus's garment. Because she pushed through the crowd, she was healed. Perseverance is what empowered Noah to continue building the ark when others mocked him. What if he'd given up?

Even when we feel like giving up, He never gives up on us. We were created to persevere. Deep within our soul, we know . . . when God encourages us to take another lap, it's because He's certain we have the inner strength to push through and press on.

Dear God,

Thank You for the gift of perseverance.
When I'm weary and my faith is weak, remind me
of the challenges You've already helped me push through,
trusting You will help me again.

Amen

The Purposed Heart

Each of you should give what you have decided in your heart to give, not reluctantly or under compulsion, for God loves a cheerful giver.

2 CORINTHIANS 9:7

Remember the saying, "It's the thought that counts?" Perhaps "thought" is the name of the seed that God plants in our heart to initiate giving with purpose.

When God's love takes root in our hearts, a fervent desire for giving begins to bloom. That desire becomes a blessing we get to give to others. From one harvest of giving to the next, heart blessings keep right on reproducing.

What a shared blessing a few dear friends and I experienced when we joined together with money and purpose to provide our very deserving mutual friend a special birthday surprise. Having never been to a spa or ridden in a limo, she was beyond thrilled when the long, white limo pulled into her driveway to pick her up. After her spa time, we met to continue her party from the limo, laughing and singing our way to many fun-filled stops along the way, and ended up at a wonderful restaurant for dinner. Far beyond the gift was the blessing of creating beautiful and lasting memories that would forever bind us together as "soul sisters."

Giving financially to a need or a cause, tending to a sick friend or family member, sending a card or care package to someone needing encouragement, and simply being present with someone in their times of sorrow are all ways we give from our heart.

Aren't you glad, when God thought of us, He purposed in His heart to give us His most cherished gift—Jesus? That's because He loved us enough to give His very best.

Dear God,

Give me a hearing heart to know what You purpose in my heart to give.
Help me pay attention to the voice in my soul that
moves me with compassion and love.

Amen

Learning to Fly

If the Son sets you free, you will be free indeed.

JOHN 8:36

Caring for our physical selves to maintain our health, well-being, and appearance serves us well in our lifetime. We fight the eventualities of time with night creams, sunscreen, and facials. We exercise, tone, and tighten and walk off calories. We hold on to what we've got for as long as possible to the best of our abilities.

Caring for our soul, in so many ways, involves just the opposite—learning to let go, breaking free from our comfort zone, taking a leap of faith into all that is unfamiliar. Allowing our soul to have control changes the dynamics of how we view the adventure of our short time here on earth. Soulful living is a gift we sometimes forget we were born with.

Like baby birds who feel the sharp twinges of discomfort as they outgrow their prickly nest, God often allows us to feel that same discomfort so intensely we finally trust that flying can't be nearly as painful as staying where we are. Our souls were born to grow and keep growing. Seek and keep seeking. Fly and keep flying.

Real freedom can't be contained or maintained. But so often we are afraid to move, change the scenery, or take the risk. We achieve real freedom when we embrace the holy wildness of our passion, our purpose, and our pilgrimage with a wild and holy God. He invites us into His great adventure—an abundant life of freedom.

Set your spirit free, and you'll begin to live. Dare to believe that the same God who teaches baby sparrows how to flap their wings will also teach us how to fly.

Dear Lord,

Take away the fear of leaving my comfort zone.

Set my soul free to soar and trust where You are leading me.

Teach me how to fly, Lord. I'm ready.

Amen

A Sacred Invitation

Sing to him, sing praise to him; tell of all his wonderful acts.
Glory in his holy name; let the hearts of those who seek the Lord rejoice.
Look to the Lord and his strength; seek his face always.
Remember the wonders he has done, his miracles,
and the judgments he pronounced.

PSALMS 105:2-5

A favorite childhood memory takes me back to summer days (and a less-threatening world) when I'd spend hours riding my old blue bicycle. Like rewinding an old movie in my mind, I warmly recall the magical feeling of peddling furiously to build up enough speed to coast downhill on the narrow, blacktopped road. When I'd fearlessly take my hands off the handlebars and stretch my arms out for balance, mimicking a bird's wings, I felt true freedom as the wind blew through my blond hair. Those were the days we found entertainment in naming cloud images and running through water sprinklers. I knew it was time to go home, or go inside, when the fireflies appeared at dusk.

Those were the days before life got complicated. As adults, we rarely feel the same bliss we experienced as a child—and not everyone had such pleasant childhood memories. Life happens, and each of us eventually experiences some form of brokenness. Those of us who have endured unspeakable loss and grief are perhaps the very ones in most need of delightful moments that can help restore our soul.

Painful experiences can't be changed, but God waits with a sacred invitation to step back into life—and embrace it again. We have the choice—to accept the invitation, to walk through God's healing gate, and to believe once again in new beginnings. If we do, perhaps we'll dare to take our hands off the handlebars, coast in the gentle breeze of God's grace, and know that somehow (perhaps by the light of fireflies), He's helping us find our way back home.

Dear God,

Teach me how to live today, in the moments of Your restoring grace.
Bring fresh hope to my soul, and help me walk in the freedom
and light of new beginnings and waiting miracles.

Amen

35

Turning Corners

**See, I am doing a new thing! Now it springs up; do you not perceive it?
I am making a way in the wilderness and streams in the wasteland.**

ISAIAH 43:19

By human nature, we want to know what's up ahead for our lives. It isn't simple curiosity that keeps us wondering; it's part of our inner security to plan and know what to expect in the days, months, and years of our future. We want a straight path, don't we? Why shouldn't we expect to travel this journey and road of life with a long, clear view?

As we process life experiences, God asks us to trust Him for what's around the next bend in the road. We don't know what to expect, but an all-knowing God does. Some corners are resting places where renewal begins to take place. Others are instructional for new plans; and some reveal an epiphany that awakens our soul. We are always aware when we've turned a corner and something new is on the horizon.

Turning corners is like taking little leaps of faith with a bit of fear and trepidation. But just beyond what is visible are landmarks of healing, surrender, trusting, dreaming, and purpose. Turning corners teaches us, molds us, and shapes us for the *new* things God is working out in our lives. With every corner turned, we'll find God is already there, waiting to be our living touchstone of hope.

Dear Heavenly Father,

When I can't see the road ahead, teach me
to trust that You are leading me by the hand.
Remind me that when I'm turning a new corner,
You are already ahead of me, waiting to encourage
my soul to keep believing in Your plan.

Amen

Unfolding

**The unfolding of your words gives light;
it gives understanding to the simple.**

PSALM 119:130

Life is made up of layers. And much like removing the layers of an onion will make us cry, so will removing the layers that cover our soul's hidden places.

A facial mask peels away layers of our skin to remove impurities and toxins. Peeling it away reveals a new layer of cleaned, toned, and glowing skin. We often layer our own souls without knowing it. Protective layers sometimes manifest as anger, bitterness, or an unwillingness to forgive. But when those layers are unfolded and peeled away, they reveal a tender and sensitive soul. We can read books, meditate, and do yoga and other spiritual practices to nourish our soul, but a vital part of real soul care is finding the truest, most vulnerable part of our being by removing the camouflaged layers and reaching into and finding the deep, secret pools of our soul's truth.

A letter that stays folded has no power. Only when it is opened, unfolded, and read does it become alive. God's Word is our living love letter from God. It's an unfolding of love, truth, and glory, opened for us to read. When He spoke of giving us abundant life, he was talking about setting our soul free from the layers of all that would keep us from receiving His gift of unconditional love. The same love that peels away the layers of shame, wounds, scars, and labels of our souls fills it with healing grace.

Dear Lord,

I invite You to peel back the layers of all that has kept my soul from living
freely and deeply and restored. Take away the pride and scars and pain
that have hidden me away from Your redemptive healing and grace.

Amen

Letting Go of Perfect

Do not set your heart on what you will eat or drink; do not worry about it.
Do not be afraid, little flock, for your Father has been pleased
to give you the kingdom.

LUKE 12:29, 32

Reality 101: Not everyone is going to like us. It's time to admit and realize that in our quest to be the best us, we are all beautiful messes. I heard someone say recently that if anyone says they have the perfect life or marriage or family, they aren't living in reality. We live messy lives that don't always make one ounce of sense. We wear our rose-colored glasses to make ourselves believe we can be all things to all people. We keep saying yes when saying no would be the wiser choice.

We create images of a perfect self we hope to project to everyone, but once we remove the masks and reveal the beautiful messiness of our human frailty, we become more comfortable with the core of who we are. Our only striving should be to simply be our best selves.

It's perfectly OK if we aren't everyone's cup of tea. Those who love us will get us—and know we're learning to be a little kinder to ourselves. Our soul finds freedom once we let go of perfect, relax, and let God use every imperfect part of us to accomplish amazing things.

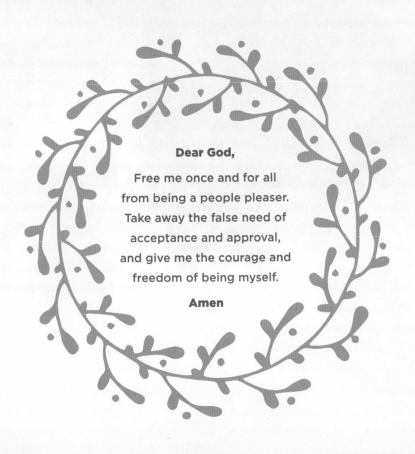

Dear God,

Free me once and for all
from being a people pleaser.
Take away the false need of
acceptance and approval,
and give me the courage and
freedom of being myself.

Amen

My Happy Place

Taste and see that the Lord is good;
blessed is the one who takes refuge in him.

PSALM 34:8

I greeted a casual friend, Debbie, recently in a grocery store checkout line. She seemed rushed to empty her basket and be on her way. I'd never seen her in a ball cap, tank top, and workout pants, but she quickly explained that she was headed to "her happy place."

When I asked her to tell me more, she smiled, explaining that her yoga class is where she connects with friends and enjoys the energizing benefits of physical stretching and other aspects of the practice.

I told her I'd been curious about possibly trying yoga, and Debbie was quick to share her revelations. After praying for God to help her find relief from debilitating arthritis, she felt prompted to call a friend who'd discovered pain management results for her own physical challenges.

"These classes have become more than a place to exercise without placing added pressure on my joints," she said. "My class time lets me practice deep breathing and helps me de-stress, mentally and spiritually. Maybe it's the release of chemical endorphins that has given me a new sense of well-being, but I have to say, I am happier when I leave my happy place—body, mind, and soul."

Yoga class will not be everyone's happy place, but we all need one, don't we? A place where we can recharge and refresh and know afterwards that we're better for having gone. Maybe it's a special park where we can organize our thoughts, a favorite rejuvenating spa, a sandy beach, a road where we prayer-walk, or a peaceful chapel. God placed a craving for peace and nourishment in our soul. And it's a blessing to know that in our greatest Happy Place—in God's presence— we can always run to find hope and renewal, and it is always waiting.

Dear God,

Knowing I can always run to You when I'm soul-tired is my true Happy Place. When I need tangible help, lead me to the place I know will energize and relax my body, mind, and spirit.

Amen

Worthy Vessels

You, Lord, are our Father. We are the clay,
you are the potter; we are all the work of your hand.

ISAIAH 64:8

The therapeutic and medicinal use of clay dates back to ancient history. Animals have even been known to use mud or clay to protect their skin from the sun or from insects. Today, considering the wide range of toxins our skin is exposed to daily, clay is a natural treatment for inflammation, impurities, and imbalances. Clay has a molecular charge that naturally seeks out toxins to bind with and draws out impurities from the surface of our skin. Also rich in beautifying minerals, clay facials give a beautiful glow for the face.

In the biblical reference to God being the Master Potter, we learn that his chief role is to unbind what is bound. Clay has no apparent value of its own; yet it can be made into objects of great value. When God is molding us, we feel the discomfort of pulling, stretching, and kneading. He uses our pliability during times of testing to knead the roughness out of our lives and hearts. He knows our souls need detoxifying in order to be our best.

The very process of molding, purifying, and removing dross shows His care and love to us. In the heat of our trials, our impurities are burned away. As our soul yields to the refining touch of His design, we become beautiful, worthy vessels.

Dear God,

Mold me and shape me into the vessel You are designing me to be.
Remove the dross from my soul that would keep me from being pliable
and usable in Your hands. You are my potter, and I am Your clay.

Amen

40

Necessary Boundaries

He gave the sea its boundary so the water would not overstep his command.

PROVERBS 8:29

We've all had those moments when we've felt someone crossed the line—a word spoken out of place or a blatant gesture of disrespect, or when a friend or loved one took us for granted. Did we speak up? Hide the hurt or anger, and pretend we didn't notice or that it was OK? Chances are, it could happen again—and unless we speak up, we're also in danger of harboring anger or bitterness.

In junior high, I had a friend whose humor bordered on being sarcastic. I began resenting how it affected me, and I cringed for others who were often the brunt of her cynicism. She thought of me as overly sensitive—and perhaps rightly so. But at some point, I had to voice my heart's truth. I also had to make a choice and set boundaries for what wasn't acceptable if we were to remain friends.

We all need boundaries, both physically and personally. They're the fences that respect, separate, and protect our soul from being overrun. Boundaries define our walk with God and our relationships, and they keep us centered and balanced. When we trust anyone, whether a friend or business contact, perimeters exist for what's expected from their viewpoint and from our own. We choose professionals we know we can trust for health care—and even to cut our hair, give a manicure, or to carefully treat our hands with hot paraffin wax. Boundaries are a form of trust for all that concerns us.

Jesus gave us boundaries to protect our soul from being wounded. Boundaries are different from walls. Walls isolate us. Boundaries free us. He taught boundaries to show what love, faith, trust, and acceptance should look like. Not all respected him, but His convictions were strong and unshakeable. Boundaries guard our truths and help us live the convictions of our soul.

Dear Lord,

Teach me to set personal boundaries and to stay within
the protective confines of the ones You have set for me.
Give me conviction to keep my boundaries strong and unshakeable.

Amen

Note to Self

A person finds joy in giving an apt reply—and how good is a timely word!

PROVERBS 15:23

I remembered reading a life-changing passage in Psalms about how David encouraged himself. I consider myself an encourager. I believe it's a gift whenever we have an opportunity to change someone's day, or perhaps life, through the power of words.

If I'm honest, there are days I'm the one in need of encouragement. I suppose it was by sheer determination that David encouraged himself through writing and expressing his deepest anguish, thoughts, and praise from the depths of his soul. Truthfully, there are days we can relate to David's transparency of words that speaks to our soul.

We all run somewhere when we are discouraged. No amount of shopping, treating ourselves, pampering, or thinking can remove the deep discouragement that settles in our soul. We just need for someone to tell us everything is going to be OK.

Some days we need a gentle reminder of "the bigger picture" in life—a fresh perspective from someone who cares. Perhaps David gave us insight into living the questions when he asked his own soul why it was so downcast. He asked, with an expectancy in his soul, for an answer from the One whose heart he was seeking. David encouraged himself. In today's language, we might use the term a "note to self." Through the writing of his songs, he found release and reminded himself that, despite his feelings, God would bring him the encouragement he needed.

God is our constant encourager—our North Star to help us find our way again. He waters our parched souls with His encouraging words of hope, renewal, and promise for every new day.

Dear Lord,

Shine Your light upon my heart and spirit, and remind me that with every new dawn, You bring fresh hope and promise for my soul.

Amen

Choosing Joy

**I have told you this so that my joy may be in you
and that your joy may be complete.**

JOHN 15:11

One of the young men who sacks my groceries each week is mentally challenged. But I can always count on Charles to lift me up when I'm down. His attitude about life and his genuine love for people shine through every compliment he gives and in all the ways he directs his praise to thanking God for the beautiful day we're having—even if it's raining. He beams with joy. Despite his disabilities, he radiates excitement for living by sharing his messages of joy with everyone he meets.

When I first met Charles, I was reminded of the words from a Bible school song I learned as a child: "I've got the joy, joy, joy, joy down in my heart . . . down in my heart to stay." The simple truth of these words is that down in our heart is where joy lives, where it finds its home—its base of operation.

The world often confuses happiness with joy. We look for feelings that bring us joy. But real joy is a knowing. Happiness is dependent on outward circumstances. Joy is not. We'll always face challenges in life we have no control over—like Charles's challenges.

Joy looks adversity in the eye and rests its head on God's chest. Jesus explained this is not the kind of joy the world knows, but a supernatural abiding peace.

Like the spa diffusers that emit a mist from essential oils that have the power to lift our mood, God's joy is the essential healing balm of joy for our soul. Joy is knowing that wherever Jesus lives, *joy* lives also . . . "down in my heart to stay."

Dear Lord,

Thank You for giving me supernatural joy that flows
like a singing river in the depths of my soul.
You are my burden bearer and my enough for all the days of my life.

Amen

Courageous Soul

Be strong and courageous. Do not be afraid; do not be discouraged, for the Lord your God will be with you wherever you go.

JOSHUA 1:9

It takes courage to start over in life—like the courageous people who have survived the devastation of a hurricane, lost a loved one, or begun a new job. It even takes personal courage to implement a new regimen, a new diet, new workout routine, or any plan to improve ourselves physically.

When we think of courage, we may think of soldiers fighting battles on the front lines or superheroes like Superman or Wonder Woman, whose daring feats of gallantry in the midst of danger save the day.

When God thinks of courage, I wonder if He thinks of courageous women like my mom, who raised nine children, or missionaries who risk their lives in unknown lands for the cause of Christ, or those who stand strong while fighting a life-threatening disease.

I wonder, when He thinks of you and me, if He remembers that time as a child when you stood up to the school bully in defense of someone you cared about or the times you did the right thing even though you could have gotten away with doing the wrong thing. When you took time to make soup for a sick friend or became someone's prayer warrior, He smiled.

When our cause is greater than our fear, courage prevails.

Every day we get up and face another day when we feel like giving up, God applauds our courage. On days when it takes courage to find a song in our heart, climb our mountains with faith, or fight for a worthy cause, we live courageously, knowing our superhero, Jesus, is with us, helping us stand and giving our courageous soul all the power and strength it needs.

Precious Lord,

How do I thank You for making me courageous?
I know, when I look to You as my source of strength and power,
You supply everything I need to prevail and win every battle I face.

Amen

The Calling

I urge you to live a life worthy of the calling you have received.

EPHESIANS 4:1

Sitting alone on a rustic cabin porch in the Ozark Mountains one summer, I sensed it stronger than ever. While a song played from my laptop, "Jesus Draw Me Ever Nearer," my tears flowed endlessly down my face as God ministered to my broken heart. My husband had just been diagnosed with a dreaded, progressive disease, and I had no idea how his life—or mine—would change.

My mountain getaway had already been planned for quite another purpose—that of resting my soul and fleshing out new plans for starting a Bible study the following month. Certainly, the news warranted cancelling my trip, but my husband insisted I go and spend some alone time processing and praying.

Seeking direction for all I should curtail in order to put my husband's needs first, I was surprised that morning at the clarity of God's voice in my soul. I knew for certain I wasn't to cancel the Bible study. Despite what lay ahead, God assured me that the calling for ministry I'd answered long ago through speaking and writing remained the same.

Callings are those stirrings in our soul that never diminish despite what we go through. They are a holy unction and commitment that beckon us onward as ambassadors to carry out a mission on His behalf. When God calls us to serve Him and others in any capacity, He strengthens and equips us to remain in the center of His will. I'm grateful today (and so is my husband) that I listened to the voice and calling in my soul that cannot be silenced.

Dear God,

Thank You for trusting me to answer the calling on my life. Give me determined trust in knowing and understanding Your divine will for my soul's journey.

Amen

Heart and Soul Friends

A friend loves at all times.

PROVERBS 17:17

Everything is more fun when shared with a friend. It's a proven fact that when we sign up for exercise classes or start a diet, teaming up with a friend will keep us on track and help us stay inspired. Going to a spa alone isn't nearly as fun as sharing the experience of therapeutic and vitalizing treatments with a friend. Who doesn't like catching up over a mani-pedi?

A friend can turn an ordinary day into a day that sparkles with adventure! A simple conversation over coffee or tea or lunch often stimulates fresh and creative ideas. I love how a dear friend always describes our time spent together as just like eating chocolate.

God knew we'd need kindred soul friends to enrich our lives and cheer us on, to awaken and inspire our deepest dreams and purpose. He knew our joy would be doubled when shared and that our souls would be healthier with the love and support of our friends in our lives.

God's divine orchestration and plan for us to journey together in life is nothing less than holy. Like dazzling light that beams warmth to our soul, the Bible reveals there may be times we'll entertain angels unaware. You don't have to look for misplaced halos or angel dust on the floor to know that an angel has been near. Just look into the eyes of the friend who brings love, beauty, and a touch of heaven to your soul.

Dear God,

Thank You for blessing
my soul with friends to share
the love, joy, and tears of
our journey together.

Amen

Divine Destiny

Who knows but that you have come to your
royal position for such a time as this?

ESTHER 4:14

Perhaps you felt it but didn't yet understand it. From the depths of your soul, you dared believe that someday, somehow you had a destiny, designed and waiting to be fulfilled.

Esther's biblical portrayal of an unlikely destiny calls us all to think outside the destiny box! She couldn't have known, as a servant girl diligently sweeping the floors of the palace, that she'd been positioned to fulfill a destiny too big to believe. Realizing that her own people outside the palace gates were doomed to die, she prayed for the right timing and opportunity to petition the king for their protection.

She prayed. She waited. She acted. She physically prepared for many months for her meeting with the king, even incorporating extravagant beauty treatments. She not only succeeded in her task, but also became the queen of the palace and a nation—a divine destiny.

Sarah carried and delivered a patriarch when she was well past childbearing age. Joseph's destiny took him from the pit to the palace. David's family saw him as a shepherd boy, but God knew he was destined to become a king.

We were in God's plan before the foundation of the earth. He planned the year, month, day, and moment we would make our entrance into this world. No one can fulfill our destiny for us. Like Esther, we can be certain God has prepared us—for such a time as this—to fulfill our soul's destiny.

Dear God,

Help me fulfill all I am here on earth to do.
Give me boldness, like Esther, and determination to help, rescue,
and make a difference in lives and in the world.

Amen

Growing Through Discipline

No discipline seems pleasant at the time, but painful.
Later on, however, it produces a harvest of righteousness
and peace for those who have been trained by it.

HEBREWS 12:11

"Discipline" is defined in the *Merriam-Webster Dictionary* as "training that corrects, molds, or perfects the mental faculties or moral character." As parents, we discipline our children primarily for their own protection and character development that will serve them throughout their lives. It's an essential and necessary part of growth.

Small children have no concept of danger, but parents know how dangerous a tiny finger in an electrical socket can be or what consequences result from tender hands touching a hot stove. Discipline is for their protection. As they grow, new levels of discipline are taught as they attend school. Learning to obey classroom rules, doing homework, and respecting their peers and leadership all require the kind of obedience *Merriam-Webster Dictionary* describes as being "compliant, conformable, and tractable."

As adults, we may think ourselves long past needing discipline, but in the spiritual sense, as well as physically and mentally, we never stop learning and growing. We have a heavenly Father who desires to protect us from danger and to make and keep us ready for all we need in life. Our experiences of discipline are for the ultimate purpose of bringing us into the character and likeness of Christ. Hebrews 12:10 explains that "God disciplines us for our good, in order that we may share in his holiness."

God loves us enough to be our parent and heavenly Father. If our spirit is sensitive and open to His instruction and correction, we can rest and trust in the security of knowing our Father knows best—and He's still keeping a protective eye on our ever-growing soul.

Dear God,

Thank You for loving me enough to speak conviction and instruction when I need it. Teach me and remind me that You are always protecting my ever-growing soul.

Amen

The Quilted Soul

You hem me in behind and before, you lay your hand upon me.

PSALM 139:5

I love quilts, especially old, antique quilts that have survived the ravages of time. Nothing warms my soul more than grabbing a cup of coffee and a quilt on a cool morning or evening to wrap up in for a little porch sitting time. Add some music and something good to read, and I have my favorite kind of down-home spa time. I can't help but wonder about the woman or women who made the quilts in my own collection. What stories and memories did they share while they sat for hours cutting and piecing together scraps from an old apron, work shirt, or outgrown piece of clothing?

One block at a time, these very old masterpieces took hours and often months to create. More important than their colors, design, and unique feel are the lives they represent.

A true quilt has three layers: a pieced top, an inner batting, and a backing. Yarn or heavy thread is worked through the layers to hold them in place and keep them from shifting. The Latin word for quilt is *culcita* and literally means "a stuffed sack." It can be used as both a noun and a verb.

Have you ever thought of your soul as a quilted masterpiece? We have a Master Quilter who faithfully stitches together the fabric and layers of our lives. With a cord not easily broken, every bright, joyous moment, every dark lament, and all the pieces and colors in between are held together by the threads of His love.

Dear God,

I trust You, the Master Quilter of my soul, to use the pieces of my life to create something beautiful. Thank You for holding every layer of my life in place.

Amen

Be Still My Soul

He leads me beside quiet waters, he refreshes my soul.

PSALMS 23:2-3

The manicurist kept reminding me to relax my fingers and keep my hands still while she was working on my nails. It wasn't time to answer my phone or grab a mint from my purse. Our fingers stay so busy; it's not easy keeping them still for very long, even when necessary. In our fast-paced society and with endless demands on our time, one of the very things we need most is time to be still. It's the only pathway that leads to the restoration and the peace our soul craves.

The psalmist David found a way to reflect and express his thankfulness for God's love, guidance, and protection, using his own shepherding experience. A shepherd's life and the ways he cares for his sheep are rich metaphors for how tenderly God cares for us. Sheep on their own will drink from muddy water and shallow pools filled with parasites. Only the shepherd knows where the still, clean, and restorative water can be found.

How often do we hurriedly search on our own for the most available, muddy water that can't possibly quench or restore us? Still waters are deep waters. Like sheep, we can't find them without our Shepherd's guidance. Once our soul gets quiet and still enough, we will find the deep waters God provides to give us the peace and restoration our soul needs. And when we sit still enough, we can get the perfect manicure.

Dear God,

Thank You for being my gentle Shepherd.
Still and quiet my spirit, and lead me to the deep,
still waters my soul needs to be healed and restored.

Amen

Soul Offerings

**Whatever you do, work at it with all your heart,
as working for the Lord, not for human masters.**

COLOSSIANS 3:23

Doesn't it feel good when you know you've done something good or given to someone? I'm not talking about a pat-on-the-back kind of feeling, but the gentle satisfaction that warms your heart knowing you gave enthusiastically, honorably, and with excellence. Anyone can go through the motions of working or giving, but when we go the extra mile or do more than what is required or expected, we're giving more than something tangible. We are giving from our soul.

When the little boy who came to hear Jesus offered his meager loaves and fishes to help feed the multitudes, he must have known there wasn't enough to go around. But from a willing heart he offered to Jesus what he had anyway; and then he watched it miraculously multiply. Perhaps Jesus saw a little soul who simply believed. His gift, in Jesus's hands, was enough.

And it was.

And it still is.

How often we diminish our talents, our gifts of time, and tiny offerings of kind words, like helping a sick friend or gifting a care package for a specific need. As we use and exercise our gifts heartily from our soul, they become a gift of honor back to Him. Soul offerings, given in His name and for His glory, will always be more than enough.

Dear Lord,

Teach me to use my gifts and humbly trust You to enlarge all that I give from my soul.

Amen

51

Go Ahead and Shine

Neither do people light a lamp and put it under a bowl.
Instead they put it on its stand, and it gives light to everyone in the house.

MATTHEW 5:15-16

How long has it been since you allowed yourself some playtime? We don't think of our adult selves as needing recess or playtime like kids do, but we need those same kind of soul breaks that help us let go of the heaviness life often heaps on us.

If we stop to think about it, most kids, when given freedom at playtime, naturally shine in their own uniqueness and spontaneity. Put us in front of a broken copy machine, and we'll fret and stress over it. Put a kid in front of one, and they may twirl around a few times, and comment, "Oh, well!" We invite stress. Kids play it away. Kids are passionate about life.

We obsess over things like toothpaste choices, credit scores, dieting, and buying Spanx and makeup. We layer our souls with concerns that dull our sparkle and our shine.

I recently noticed after using a homemade lemon juice treatment on my face how much brighter my skin looked. The citric acid dissolved away the dullness I didn't even realize was covering my skin. When we ask God to dissolve the stress and worries that dull our soul, His light and glory will shine much brighter through us.

The next time you feel anxious or weighed down with the worries of adulthood, stop, twirl around, take a little soul break, and sing the familiar childhood song, "This little light of mine, I'm gonna let it shine." Remember the blessing and freedom we're given to let His glory and light shine through us. Since that's what we were created to do, go ahead and shine!

Dear Lord,

Shine through me. Make my life a stream of Your light for all the world to see.

Amen

Flowers for My Soul

See how the flowers of the field grow. They do not labor or spin.
Yet I tell you not even Solomon in all his splendor
was dressed like one of these.

MATTHEW 6:28-29

For several months, I'd been searching for ways to slow down and simplify my life. It required concentrating on the real value of time and being more aware of how I spent each day. A season of overbooked engagements, stress, and burnout left me pondering priorities and goals.

On a rare day with no pressing duties, I ventured into town to run a few errands. Driving a little slower on that sunny morning, I noticed a field of wild sunflowers near the road. I pulled over and got out of the car to take a closer look. Another car pulled over behind me, and I could see it was a friend I'd not seen in a long time.

"What are you doing out here?" she asked.

"Well, I guess I'm about to pick some of these flowers," I answered. "I can't resist. They just look like happiness to me!"

The little things in God's creation that call to our soul should never be passed up. They have their own language our soul understands. Slow down. Enjoy God's bounty and the beauty He's given us to enjoy. His wayside florist is always open—and free for the picking.

When I went back home that day, it wasn't my purchases from the store that mattered. It was the free gift from God's bounty that I was most proud of. My soul was filled with a sense of worship as I placed the bright yellow sunflowers in a vase. I wondered if He was pleased I'd taken the time to notice and harvest the beautiful flowers He'd provided for my soul.

Dear Lord,

Thank You for the gifts of beauty
and nature that often go unnoticed.
Help me take the time to enjoy the little things of life
that brighten and nourish my soul.

Amen

Creative Awakening

We have different gifts, according to the grace given to each of us.

ROMANS 12:6

Deep within your soul lies a wealth of creative potential.

"Create" means "to bring into existence, to produce through imaginative skill," according to *Merriam-Webster Dictionary*. Creativity is one of the most important parts of your soul journey. No one can tell your story, write your songs or poetry, paint the flowers, or bring life to the thoughts and ideas that are part of you.

The adult coloring book craze became so popular because we realized we never outgrew our need to create. Our soul longs to express and find the freedom that came so naturally as a child. God loves color! And He placed a need for it in our souls to help us live fully alive.

I daresay our creativity is possibly our deepest form of worship. Art workshops are even finding their way into the church. Enjoying social activities with others releases the oxytocin chemical in our brain that produces a sense of well-being.

We were created to create! It's like electricity—and it brings light. And it's never too late. At age 79, Oliver Wendell Holmes, Sr. wrote *Over the Teacups*. Tennyson wrote "Crossing the Bar" at age 83. Goethe completed *Faust* at 80. Verdi composed his famous "Ave Maria" at 85.

Today's technology certainly has its purpose, but our souls have long been starved for an organic way to express our soul and connect with the Creator.

It's the perfect way for your creative soul to rise up, express itself, and spread its wings.

Dear God,

Paint Your love and beauty
across the canvas of my soul.
Color it with the joy and freedom
of creativity You've given me to enjoy
and share with others.

Amen

Surrendered Trust

**Trust in the Lord with all your heart
and lean not on your own understanding.**

PROVERBS 3:5

How often do we try to figure things out first before we go to God and pray? Even in our declarations of faith, our human nature is to look for formulas. Perhaps it's some multistep program that will guarantee results or a mantra of spoken words that we hope will somehow assure victory over certain situations.

As individuals, we have our own unique physical and spiritual needs. If we go to a health spa, we surrender our trust for a determined customized treatment—just for us. There are no cut-in-stone formulas that are used to get the results we hope for.

God's ways are beyond what we can comprehend, and His thoughts are higher than our own. In fact, He rarely works things out the way we think He will. He customizes and works out the details of our life and answers our prayers in ways that will prove it is Him—and nothing we could've planned—that gets us through.

He works in ways that leave us awestruck, humbled, and surprised over and over again by His sovereign glory.

Trusting Him, fully surrendered, brings the kind of peace to our striving souls that is beyond our human understanding. But our surrendered souls become the doors He walks right into—where He personally reveals His great love, mercy, and wisdom.

Dear Lord,

Teach me to pray first instead of trying to figure out things on my own. You have the best plan for my life—and every situation—so help me trust my life and my soul to Your answers.

Amen

A Kindness Remembrance

But when the kindness and love of God our Savior appeared,
he saved us, not because of the righteous things we had done,
but because of his mercy.

TITUS 3:4-5

When a friend called to say she needed some time and space to rest her soul, I offered a guest room, with all the alone time she needed. On the second day, she shared a scrapbooking project she was putting together in remembrance of her son who had passed away. Her favorite entries were handwritten letters and printed e-mails she'd requested various people who knew him to send. Each had agreed to perform a random act of kindness in his name and send a letter describing their experience.

A one-year anniversary of such sorrow was remembered by celebrating life—and reaching out to others. An opened door, a kind note tucked into a windshield wiper, a gift card to a stranger, and the housebound woman who fed a stray cat—all stories of unexpected mercy performed in memory of my friend's son.

It's our kindness that changes hearts and ultimately changes the world.

We encumber our soul's mission if we believe our tiny offerings don't matter—that unless we can do big things, we shouldn't attempt anything. Perhaps the greatest legacy we can ever hope for is to be remembered for our kindness. We are a candle of mercy and love—to one or many—shining forth God's kindness and unconditional love, right where we are.

Dear God,

Let kindness always be alive in my soul—
ready to help and reach out, with the same
tender mercy You have given me.

Amen

Faith Lessons

**Faith is confidence in what we hope for
and assurance about what we do not see.**

HEBREWS 11:1

One sunny afternoon, I decided to condition my hair and do my nails while catching a few sunrays from my deck. It's not easy to carve out time for those needed regimens, but that day, I also used the time for reflection and prayer.

A few feet from my lounge chair, I noticed a lizard with a very long tail running along the deck railing. I couldn't help but think that at any moment, one of the curious outdoor cats would certainly grab that long tail.

I smiled and said, "Thank you, God, for using that lizard today." You see, when a lizard loses his tail, he just grows a new one! That day, I needed the faith of a lizard to know that no matter what I was lacking, God would supply and provide.

Faith is like coming to the edge of a cliff, knowing that if we fall, God will either catch us or teach us to fly on the way down. Faith is stepping out on nothing and landing on something. We don't see the wind, but we see what it moves and touches.

While the warmth of the sun conditioned my hair, God conditioned my soul and reminded me of a few truths. Like the faith of a lizard, I know God has my back—or tail!

Dear God,

When my faith needs refreshing, remind me of Your faithfulness through unexpected lessons You use to help me believe.

Amen

Blue-Plate Special

I thank my God every time I remember you.

PHILIPPIANS 1:3

We'd changed our plans for a girls' day out several times in the past few months. We simply had too much on our plates to take the time. But today was finally the day. We were getting together to go to a nearby town known for its unique shops, boutiques, and cafés. We needed a soul-to-soul kind of day to relax and catch up on each other's lives, and a change of scenery couldn't hurt.

As we enjoyed our blue-plate lunch special, I could feel my soul unwinding, calming, and silently saying thank you. I'd missed my friend. I'd missed her wit and wisdom and transparency. I'd missed a little bit of life that I didn't want to neglect again.

There will always be something pressing we need to handle. There will always be too few hours with an impossible list begging our attention. But there will not always be one more chance to spend time with our friends or loved ones. When that time is gone, nothing on our to-do lists will matter.

We choose how we spend or waste our gift of time. When all is said and done, the memories made with someone we love will be our most priceless and lasting treasures.

If you have something good to say, say it now. If you have someone to love, love them now. Share the joy and tears. Unload your always-too-full plate and make room for the blue-plate special moments of life that will feed your soul.

Dear God,

Thank You for the blessing of time—and for teaching me
to keep time spent with friends and loved ones a priority.
Help me never get so busy that I miss my life.

Amen

Transformed

**The Lord will create a new thing on earth—
the woman will return to the man.**

JEREMIAH 31:22

When we met for breakfast one morning, my friend brought her new journal with her. She laid it on the table and began telling me why the typed label on the front of the colorful cover read, "Transformed." The first pages were lists of all the things she wanted to change in her life, including physical, health, and spiritual changes. The next few pages were written plans for incorporating the changes. As if some mysterious happening had occurred, she leaned over her coffee cup and whispered, "I can feel my life changing. Body, mind, and spirit—it's amazing how they all work together. The very first change was giving myself permission to take care of me."

Thumbing through her journal, I saw the word "exfoliate" at the top of one page. Beneath it was a cutout recipe from a magazine for a sugar facial scrub. The short article explained that for skin cell renewal to take place, the top layers of rough, dry, or dead skin need to be exfoliated. Afterwards, more pliable and softer skin absorbs moisturizers to more deeply replenish, nourish, and condition.

There are times in our lives when we'll feel like everything is being stripped away from our soul—and even though it hurts, we can trust that we are being prepared for what we are still becoming. There are many biblical accounts of those who encountered the transforming power of Christ. When they allowed the rough, dead layers of their soul to be sloughed away, grace appeared. Change is always uncomfortable at first, but fully inviting God to transform us prepares our soul to deeply receive the soaking, renewing nourishment of His love.

Dear God,

Take away anything that keeps my heart and soul

from receiving the fresh nourishment of Your love and grace.

Transform me and continue to renew my spirit.

Amen

Just Breathe

**The Spirit of God has made me;
the breath of the Almighty gives me life.**

JOB 33:4

Juice bars and coffee bars are common in most cities today. But even more recently, oxygen bars are popping up in U.S. health spas and in Canada and Japan where it is believed they originated to help people overcome the effects of air pollution. People who pay for oxygen delivered through a mask worn over their faces say the oxygen boosts their energy, provides stress relief, eases headaches, and increases exercise endurance.

While there is no scientific evidence documenting the benefits of casual oxygen therapy, there is proof of medical benefits from practicing deep breathing. There are even certain guided exercises that teach methods of inhaling, holding the breath, and slowly exhaling.

Tension from prolonged stress affects us physically, emotionally, and spiritually. We all go through situations and seasons of stress where we feel we can barely breathe, much less relax and exhale. Inhaling and exhaling seem like a common thing. But that's what keeps us alive.

A favorite praise song talks about God being the very air we breathe. And sometimes breathing in His presence is the best prayer we can pray. With no words, we silently ask Him to breathe life into us. Oxygenate our soul. Breathing in, believing He is the giver of every breath, is a holy way of communicating that He is everything we need. And on days our soul is gasping for air, we can remind ourselves to just breathe—deeply, slowly, and prayerfully. As we feel the tension release physically, our soul exhales, restful in grateful praise.

Dear God,

There are times I'm so desperate for You, I feel like I'm holding my breath,
waiting for peace, waiting for an answer, waiting to exhale.
Teach me to just breathe in Your presence, learn to exhale every care and concern,
and rest in Your peace.

Amen

Beautiful Fragrance

For we are to God the pleasing aroma of Christ among those who are being saved and those who are perishing.

2 CORINTHIANS 2:15

I love the smell of coffee brewing in the morning, and how the aroma of a simmering pot of homemade stew creates a sense of comfort. Apple pies or cookies baking in the oven make a home smell warm and cozy. Light an evergreen-scented candle, and Christmas memories arise. Apple-cider-scented candles remind me of autumn. These are aromas I love. When I'm ready to do some serious house cleaning, I simmer my own homemade orange-cinnamon marmalade oils in a small pot on my stove, and I feel a heightened sense of energy.

We were created to respond to the sense of smell on an emotional level more strongly than with any other sense. A single aroma can induce feelings and trigger forgotten memories, something that involves the limbic system and a complex process associated with the smell and memory area of the brain.

Aromatherapy, dating back thousands of years, is still widely used today. Most day spas use diffused essential oils to revive, calm, relax, energize, and uplift both mind and body and to create a tranquil atmosphere. Just as beautiful scents invite and entice a sense of well-being, unpleasant scents make us want to distance ourselves from them.

The Bible describes our relationship with Christ, evident in our actions and attitudes, as a pleasing aroma that spreads His love and goodness to others. It's a fragrance that can't be bought or manufactured. We are encouraged to live a life of love, "just as Christ loved us and gave himself up for us as a fragrant offering and sacrifice to God." Ephesians 5:2

To know that our lives are like a lovely, lingering fragrance to God and to others is a beautiful, humbling, and powerful thought to ponder.

Dear Lord,

**May my life be a sweet fragrance, pleasing to You,
and the evidence that makes others want to know You more.**

Amen

Feedback

If you enjoyed this book
or it has touched your life in some way,
we'd love to hear from you.

Please write a review at Hallmark.com,
e-mail us at booknotes@hallmark.com,
or send your comments to:

Hallmark Book Feedback
P.O. Box 419034
Mail Drop 100
Kansas City, MO 64141

About the Author

Susan Duke is a wife, mother, motivational speaker, singer, and an inspirational writer, author and coauthor of seventeen books.

Susan travels, speaking for Christian conferences, retreats, and seminars, corporations, national teachers' associations, community groups, writing conferences (including her own "Writing With Wings" Seminars), and churches of all denominations. An enthusiastic communicator and true encourager, Susan combines humor, sensitivity, transparency, and poignant biblical truth in all of her messages. Her compelling testimony of God's restoration after tragedy offers a bridge of hope for hurting hearts.

Susan's passion for teaching includes her local "God's Porch Bible Study," where a growing number of ladies meet each month to discover a deeper, more joyful, and adventurous walk with Christ.

In 2002, Susan founded the Grieving Forward outreach and support group in her community for anyone experiencing loss. The meetings offer a safe place for grieving hearts to gather and find hope, solace, and support.

Susan and her husband, Harvey, reside in East Texas.